Anglo-Saxons

c. 450	First settlements in Kent and East Anglia
597	Saint Augustine converts King Ethelbert of Kent
600	Anglo-Saxons control most of England
625	A king is buried at Sutton Hoo
635	Aidan founds Lindisfarne
c.650	King Penda seizes Mercia
670	Edwin is king of Northumbria
688	King Caedwalla of Wessex goes to Rome
731	Bede writes his *History*
760	Offa builds a dyke between England and Wales
793	The Danes raid Lindisfarne
878	Alfred makes a treaty with the Danes
991	The battle of Maldon in Essex
994	King Sweyn leads the Danish raids
1016	Canute the Dane becomes king of England
1042	Edward the Confessor is crowned
1066	The Normans seize England from the Anglo-Saxons

Anglo-Saxons

Margaret Sharman

Evans Brothers Limited

BRITAIN THROUGH THE AGES

First published in this edition in 2003 by
Evans Brothers Limited
2A Portman Mansions
Chiltern St
London W1U 6NR

First published in hardback in 1995
© Margaret Sharman 1995

Published in paperback in 1995. Reprinted 1995.

Printed in Belgium

A catalogue record for this book is available from
the British Library.

ISBN 0 237 52571 2

Acknowledgements
Design: Ann Samuel
Editorial: Nicola Barber
Illustrations: Nick Hawken and Mike White
Production: Jenny Mulvanny

Acknowledgements

For permission to reproduce copyright material,
the author and publishers gratefully acknowledge
the following:

Cover: (main) the art archive, (background) The
Ancient Art & Architecture Collection, (top & bot-
tom) The Bridgeman Art Library, (middle) Saint
Edmundsbury Borough Council/West Stow
Anglo-Saxon Village Trust. Title page
R.Sheridan/The Ancient Art & Architecture
Collection. page 6 (top) British Library,
London/The Bridgeman Art Library, (bottom)
York Archaeological Trust Historical Picture
Library. page 7 York Archaeological Trust
Historical Picture Library, (bottom) Musée Conde,
Chantilly/Giraudon/The Bridgeman Art Library.
page 8 (top) R.Sheridan/The Ancient Art &
Architecture Collection, (bottom) Henry
McInnes/Still Moving Picture Company. page 9
R.Sheridan/The Ancient Art & Architecture
Collection. page 10 The British Museum,
London/The Bridgeman Art Library. page 11
Michael Holford. page 13 Archie Miles. page 14
the art archive. page 15 British Library,
London/The Bridgeman Art Library. page 16 The
Dean and Chapter of Durham. page 16 (top)
Hunting Aerofilms Limited, (bottom) the art
archive/Ashmoleam Museum, Oxford. page 17
(top) Michael Holford, (bottom) British Library,
London/The Bridgeman Art Library. page 18
Private Collection/The Bridgeman Art Library.
page 19 (top) The Ancient Art & Architecture
Collection, (bottom) The Bodleian Library, Oxford
(MS Hattom 20, fol.2r). page 20 Saint
Edmundsbury Borough Council/West Stow
Anglo-Saxon Village Trust, (bottom) Manfred
Danegger, NHPA. page 22 (top) British Library,
London/The Bridgeman Art Library, (bottom)
Michael Holford. page 23 (top) York
Archaeological Trust Historical Picture Library.
page 24 (top) B Norman/The Ancient Art
&Architecture Collection, (bottom) Michael
Holford. page 25 R.Sheridan/The Ancient Art &
Architecture Collection. page 26 (top)
R.Sheridan/The Ancient Art & Architecture
Collection, (bottom) David O'Connor. page 27
(top) Mary Evans Picture Library, (bottom) the art
archive/British Museum. page 28 R.Sheridan/The
Ancient Art & Architecture Collection. page 29
Musée de la Tapisserie, Bayeux/With special
authorisation of the City of
Bayeux/Giraudon/The Bridgeman Art Library.

Contents

The Anglo-Saxons arrive

Nearly 1,600 years ago, foreigners from Western Europe started to invade Britain. They came from pagan tribes known as the Angles, the Saxons and the Jutes. The Angles settled in East Anglia, the east midlands and the north east; the Saxons went in to the south and the Jutes settled in Kent and the Isle of Wight. We call them all the Anglo-Saxons. Their kings ruled Britain for over 500 years.

Before the Anglo-Saxons came, England and Wales formed one prosperous Christian country. It had been ruled by the Romans for 450 years. But the Roman army left when Rome itself was invaded. So the Anglo-Saxons were able to raid a land that had no proper defences.

Bede, writing his *Life of St. Cuthbert.* Behind him is the monastery at Jarrow, Northumbria, where he worked.

How do we know about the Anglo-Saxons?

At this time, very few people could read or write. Most of the writing was done by monks. Some of the books the monks wrote have survived to this day. A monk called Bede, who lived from AD 673 to 735, wrote a history of England. He also wrote about the lives of famous monks and bishops. A bishop called Asser wrote about King Alfred. Later, various other histories were joined together. We call this book *The Anglo-Saxon Chronicles.* It is more about kings and battles than about ordinary people.

We know more about ordinary people from archaeology. Archaeologists have dug up Anglo-Saxon villages and cemeteries. They have found traces of the clothes people wore and objects that they used. These things help us to understand what life was like in Anglo-Saxon times.

Archaeologists working at the site of a building from the 10th century

What happened to the British?

When the Anglo-Saxons invaded, the British people fought fiercely for their land for more than 100 years. Some of them were pushed westwards. They settled in Wales and in Cornwall. The British spoke a Celtic language, which was like the modern Welsh. Until recently, Cornish people spoke a similar language. Others crossed the English Channel to Brittany, which was named after their homeland, Britain. The Breton language is similar to Welsh and Cornish.

There were pagan people called Picts living in Scotland. Most of their land was never occupied by the Anglo-Saxons.

The Anglo-Saxons fought with bows, arrows and spears. These iron spear heads were buried underground for hundreds of years.

King Arthur

This picture shows the famous King Arthur and his knights, sitting at the Round Table. Although the legends about him were made up hundreds of years later, there may really have been a British leader called Arthur who fought against the Anglo-Saxons. King Arthur was said to have been very brave. Later writers said that he had once killed 'a giant of marvellous bigness' and, in a battle, 'he alone' killed 960 Anglo-Saxons. The legend says that Arthur had a magician at his court called Merlin. Arthur's knights did many brave deeds. There is a story that they searched for a lost Christian cup called the Holy Grail. It is said that Jesus had used this cup at the Last Supper. You can see the Grail on the table in this picture.

Pagans and Christians

The figure on this bronze disk may be a pagan god with a snake.

The religion of the invaders

The invaders had many pagan gods. Woden ruled the Sun and the sky. Freya was the goddess of love, Thor made thunder and lightning, and Tiw was the god of war. The Anglo-Saxons believed that these four helped them to conquer the British. Their descendants held these beliefs until they became Christians.

> 📖 **Words, words, words ....**
>
> Some of our weekdays are named after the Anglo-Saxons' pagan gods:
> Tuesday was Tiw's Day; Wednesday was Woden's Day;
> Thursday was Thor's Day; and Friday was Freya's Day.

Christianity spreads from Ireland

Soon after the Romans left Britain, a young man called Patrick was captured by pirates. They took him to Ireland as a slave. He escaped from Ireland and became a Christian priest. In about 435 he returned there as a bishop. He is Saint Patrick, the patron saint of Ireland.

The Irish Christians built monasteries in Ireland. There was also a famous one on the island of Iona, far away from the pagan Anglo-Saxons.

Iona as it is today. The cross is Celtic but the buildings form part of an abbey rebuilt there in 1203, nearly 800 years ago.

The monks wore rough woollen clothes and leather sandals. They worked in the fields, growing crops and tending cattle. They studied, and copied the Gospels. Their books were beautifully illustrated. They used gold and silver leaf as well as coloured paints.

In 635 Aidan, a monk from Iona, set up a monastery at Lindisfarne, an island off the coast of Northumbria. Here the monks made a wonderful illustrated book which we know as the Lindisfarne Gospels. Its colours are almost as bright today as when they were painted.

This page of the Lindisfarne Gospels shows that scribes took great pride in their work. Each page took many days to complete.

Christianity spreads from Kent

In 597 Pope Gregory sent a monk named Augustine from Rome to Britain. He landed in Kent with 40 monks. His task was to convert the Anglo-Saxons to Christianity. Ethelbert, the King of Kent, and Queen Bertha welcomed them. Bertha came from France, and was already a Christian. Augustine persuaded Ethelbert to be baptised with all his courtiers. Ethelbert built churches, and appointed priests.

Under Ethelbert's protection, Augustine and his monks travelled all over England preaching. They were not always successful. Sometimes the people they converted went back to their pagan ways. It was over 100 years before the whole of England was a Christian country again. Kent is the home of the Archbishop of Canterbury. The first Archbishop was Augustine himself.

It became important for monks and nuns to learn to read the Bible and other Christian books. In about 670 Abbot Adrian of Canterbury was the head of a school for priests and monks. The young men were taught Greek and Latin, religion and law. Students came from all over England and Ireland. One of Adrian's pupils, Aldhelm, wrote poetry in Old English. The poems were sung to harp music which guided people to church.

Is it true?

There is a story that, one day, some Anglo-Saxon slaves were being sold in the market place in Rome. Pope Gregory was told they were pagan Angles. 'No,' he said, 'not Angles, but angels.'

Five English kingdoms

The early Anglo-Saxon period is part of the 'Dark Ages' – a time when most people could not read or write. We have learned what we know about the Dark Ages from archaeology. We know that the Anglo-Saxon settlers cleared the forests to make farm land. Family groups joined together and formed settlements. In time, groups of settlements were ruled by powerful lords who called themselves kings. There were many kingdoms. For 300 years they fought one another for land and power. In the west, they raided the kingdoms of Wales, and the Welsh raided the Anglo-Saxon farms for cattle. When an Anglo-Saxon kingdom became very powerful, other kingdoms had to pay tribute.

Bede, the monk, wrote down a list of the most important kings in England. He calls them 'bretwaldas'. They included Ethelbert of Kent, Redwald of East Anglia and kings Edwin, Oswald and Oswy of Northumbria. Here Bede's list ends, though we know that later kings were just as powerful as these.

East Anglia

We know very little about the kingdom of East Anglia, except that it had busy ports, and the people traded with Sweden.

This is the top of a sceptre found at Sutton Hoo. The sceptre is made of very smooth stone. There are eight faces carved on it, four at each end. On top is an iron ring, and the bronze figure of a stag.

This gold lid closed the king's purse. It is decorated with coloured glass and precious stones. The purse contained gold coins which had been minted (made) in France.

A solid gold buckle fastened the king's cloak on his shoulder. It is decorated with a design of snakes and other animals.

In 1939 archaeologists made an important discovery. At Sutton Hoo in Suffolk they uncovered a barrow (a great mound of earth). An important king, perhaps Bede's 'bretwalda' Redwald, had been buried there. When he died in about 625, his body was laid in a long and graceful boat. Inside the boat were hundreds of beautiful objects. Many of them had been made in France, or even in Egypt and the Middle East. The king's helmet came from Sweden. With it were a sceptre, silver bowls, ivory drinking horns, precious jewellery, and a lyre (a musical instrument). The discovery shows us how rich the Anglo-Saxon kings were. It also tells us a great deal about crafts, weapons and trade with other countries. This is the only burial of its kind found in England. Later, Christian kings were buried in churches or cathedrals.

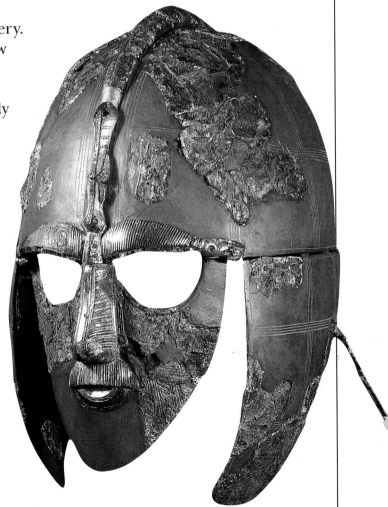

In battle King Redwald wore this decorated iron helmet. When it was found, it had been broken into tiny pieces. Scholars have put it back together. The eyebrows are made of silver wires. There are red garnets over the eye holes. The helmet was probably padded with leather, like a crash-helmet today.

Kent

When Saint Augustine landed there in 597 the kingdom of Kent was very powerful. King Ethelbert's father-in-law was the king of Paris and there was much trade between the two kingdoms. Many luxury items came by sea for the rich and powerful king and his lords. The king's palace and church were at Canterbury.

Wessex

In the west of England, a fierce young man called Caedwalla made himself king of the kingdom of Wessex. He killed the king of Sussex, and captured the Isle of Wight. He may have ruled Kent as well. Surprisingly, this warlike king became friendly with a monk from Northumbria called Wilfred. He gave Wilfred some of his new lands in the Isle of Wight and Wilfred built a monastery there.

   The people of Wessex were amazed when, in 688, Caedwalla gave up the throne. He went to Rome, and was baptised by the Pope. Soon afterwards he became ill and died. He was buried in his white baptism robe in St Peter's Church. He was about 30 years old.

Northumbria

The land 'north of the Humber' – Northumbria – was the largest kingdom. It included part of Scotland. When Edwin became king, in 670, Northumbria was the most advanced kingdom and King Edwin had a fine palace at Yeavering, near Bamburgh.

   The countryside was peaceful. Along the rough stone roads, bronze cups were hung from posts, so that travellers could drink from the streams and springs. Fishermen and traders worked on the west and east coasts.

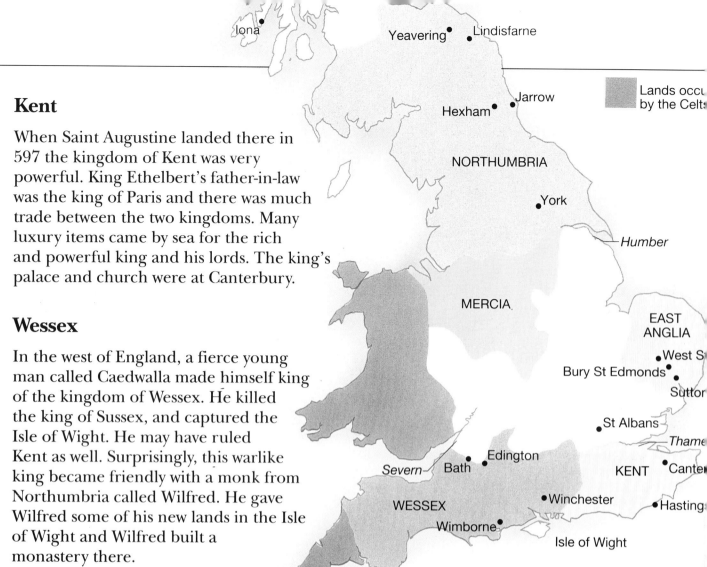

The kingdoms have no proper boundaries, as they were always changing. This map shows some of the places you can read about in this book.

A woman could carry her new-born babe across the island from sea to sea without any fear of harm.

Bede

Northumbria had many important places of learning. King Edwin and his sons gave a great deal of money to the monastery at Jarrow. Northumbria became the most learned place in England.

Mercia

Meanwhile, a pagan war leader named Penda at last defeated the Christian British who were living in central England. We call his kingdom Mercia. Later kings of Mercia were just as warlike. They gained control over most of southern England, including East Anglia and Kent.

In 757 Offa was king of Mercia. He invaded Wessex and forced its king into exile. The king of East Anglia went to visit him because he wanted to marry Offa's daughter and Offa killed him. Few Anglo-Saxon kings died naturally. Sometimes they were killed in battle; sometimes they were killed by their own lords. But this killing shocked people because it was very violent and unexpected. In Offa's reign, young men spent most of their time fighting. They invaded Wales, Wessex, Northumbria, Kent and East Anglia.

This is Offa's Dyke, a great ditch along his western border of England. Offa had the dyke dug by thousands of men, as a boundary between the English and the Welsh. The earth taken from the ditch was piled high. The bank may have had a wooden fence built on top of it. No man on horseback could cross such a boundary.

The fury of the Northmen

The Anglo-Saxons used to pray 'From the fury of the Northmen, good Lord deliver us.' The 'Northmen' were the pagan Danes. They were also called Vikings, which means pirates or sea-raiders. Every summer they came to raid the British Isles. The Anglo-Saxons paid them thousands of pounds to go away but this only encouraged them to come back again.

In 793 there were storms and strange sights at Lindisfarne. People said this was a sign that bad times were coming. Sure enough, the Danes soon invaded Lindisfarne monastery. The Danes stole precious objects and burnt the beautiful manuscripts. They killed most of the monks and sold the rest as slaves.

Is it true?

There is a legend that one day Alfred sheltered in a cowman's house. The cowman's wife asked him to watch the cakes she was baking. Alfred forgot the cakes, and they were burnt. When the woman returned she scolded Alfred, not realising that he was her king.

> *... fierce, foreboding omens came over the land of Northumbria, and wretchedly terrified the people. There were whirlwinds, lightning storms, and fiery dragons were seen flying in the sky.*
>
> The Anglo-Saxon Chronicle

In 865 hundreds of Danes landed on the east coast of England. They wore padded leather clothing and wolfskins, which made them look fierce and frightening. They killed many people with bows and arrows and swords. This time, the Danes had come to settle in England. Over the next few years they conquered Northumbria, Mercia and East Anglia. By 877, they had reached Wessex. Alfred, the king of Wessex, had to retreat to Somerset. At Athelney, an island

The Danes built excellent ships. At the front of the ship was a high prow, sometimes carved with a dragon's head. Each ship carried about 30 men. They hung their round shields over the ship's side.

DANELAW

This map shows where the Danelaw was. England was now divided into two kingdoms. The Danes called their towns by Danish names.

surrounded by marshes, he built a fort. Many warriors joined him. They left the island by a secret path and, in 878, after a fierce battle, they defeated the Danish army at Edington.

(Alfred) closed his ranks, shield locked with shield, and fought fiercely against the entire heathen host in long and stubborn stand.

Asser

T*hen the force (the Danes) gave him hostages, and great oaths that they would go from his kingdom; they also promised that their king would receive baptism.*

The Anglo-Saxon Chronicle

This picture shows St. Cuthbert. He is being visited by the king, who is asking him to become Bishop of Lindisfarne.

The Danes signed a treaty with Alfred. They agreed to stay in Northumbria, part of Mercia and East Anglia. This region became known as the Danelaw. Some of the Danish settlers married Anglo-Saxon women.

St Cuthbert, a famous monk, died in 687 at Lindisfarne. When the Danes invaded the island, some monks managed to escape with St Cuthbert's coffin. In the coffin were Bede's copy of St John's Gospel, a silver cross, and this ivory comb. The saint was finally laid to rest in Durham.

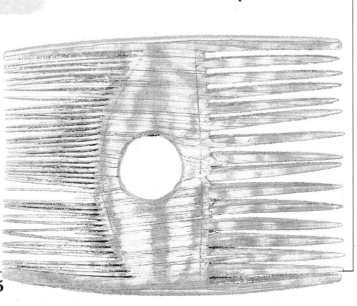

Alfred the Great

Today, Winchester's street pattern is the same as it was in King Alfred's time. Inside the old Roman wall, the streets are in a grid pattern, crossing one another.

Once the Danes had been defeated, King Alfred could concentrate on ruling his kingdom. He built fortified towns, called burhs, in western England. In times of trouble, the burhs gave protection to people living in nearby villages. Burhs included Southwark (near London), Worcester, Oxford and Winchester, which was Alfred's capital. Inside the walls at Winchester there were palaces for the king and the bishop. There was a church where the kings of Wessex were crowned and buried. People went to the burhs to buy and sell their produce and they became important market centres. A burh was allowed to mint its own coins.

In Alfred's reign, the army was well organised. Half of it patrolled the borders of the kingdom. The other half stayed at home. These soldiers were the reserve army. They could be called out when they were needed. Alfred also built ships to prevent other Danes from reaching the English coast.

The Danes had killed the educated monks who had copied manuscripts in Latin. The young men who took their place could not read Latin. Alfred wanted them to have books written in English. He had taught himself to read and write. He translated the Psalms and the Lord's Prayer, and other religious works, into English. Very few people could read or write and Alfred encouraged his people to learn.

Alfred died in 899, having ruled for 28 years. Because of his bravery, his learning and his sensible rule he is known as Alfred the Great.

Words, words, words ....

Our word 'borough' comes from the Anglo-Saxon 'burh'.

This jewel belonged to King Alfred the Great. Round the edge are the words 'Alfred had me made'.

The Danes return

King Alfred's son and grandson ruled well but the Danes were soon making trouble again. The English paid them to stay within the Danelaw but they wanted the whole of England. Other Danes started raiding from Denmark. In 991 they defeated an English army at Maldon in Essex. They destroyed Ipswich, which was an important port. In 994, the Danish king, Sweyn, led raids on England. In 1013 he made himself king of the Danelaw. He marched to London to fight the English King Ethelred the Unready. Ethelred's wife, Emma, was a daughter of the Duke of Normandy so the royal family fled to France.

> **A** shout went up in that place; ravens circled round,
> the eagle, eager for carrion: the world was in uproar ...
> Bows were busy, shield clashed with point.
> Bitter was the battle rush – warriors fell
> on either side, young men lay still.
>
> From an Anglo-Saxon poem about the Battle of Maldon

Is it true?

It is said that Canute's councillors flattered him. They said he could do anything, even stop the tide coming in. Canute was tired of their flattery. His servants took his throne down to the seashore. When the tide came in, he proved to them that his feet got just as wet as everybody else's!

A few years later Ethelred's son, Edmund Ironside, lost a great battle against the Danes in Essex. He had to sign a treaty with Sweyn's son Canute. They were to share the country between them. When Edmund died soon afterwards, Canute became king of all England. To please the English, he married Queen Emma.

Canute appointed leaders in Wessex, Mercia, and Northumbria. These leaders were called earls and they helped Canute to rule. They all had armies and they became very powerful. Canute died in 1035 and his two Danish sons ruled after him. After they died, Ethelred's son Edward the Confessor became king.

This is King Canute, wearing his crown and holding a sceptre.

Words, words, words ....

Ethelred's nickname 'the Unready' doesn't mean that he wasn't ready but that he was unwise, or 'un-raedy'.

The King and his people

Edward the Confessor is crowned in 1043. The Archbishop is pouring oil on his head as a sign that he is the rightful king.

A king of all England was crowned by the Archbishop of Canterbury. The king swore to rule justly and peacefully. He was given a ring and a sword. After the ceremony the people shouted 'Long live the king!'

The lords were very powerful and were often very rich. The king had to be sure of their loyalty, so he made them swear an oath to be true to him alone. They had to provide soldiers if the king needed an army. Three times a year the king met his lords. If a lord failed to come, the king became suspicious. Kings never felt safe – and many died a violent death.

The king chose the most important bishops and lords to help him rule. They were called the Witan. He consulted them about important matters. King Ine of Wessex (688-725) appointed officials called ealdormen to govern different parts of his kingdom. This was the beginning of local government.

England became one kingdom under King Canute. He divided the land into 'hundreds' for good government. About 12 hundreds made a shire. Shires were much the same as our counties. Each shire was governed by a 'shire reeve' or sheriff. The sheriff collected taxes, and saw that people kept the law.

Keeping the law

The earliest written laws we know about come from Kent, in the 600s. Other kingdoms then wrote down their own laws. King Alfred's law code brought the laws of the different kingdoms up to date. As well as deciding on punishments, they gave rules for buying and selling.

The king himself dealt with really serious crimes. He could take away a lord's land or have him executed.

Ordinary people were tried in courts in their own hundred or shire. The most common crimes were cattle stealing and theft. Very poor people sometimes became robbers, or even joined the Danes. If they were caught they could be hanged, whipped or have their little fingers cut off.

If someone was killed, his family had the right to kill the murderer. This often started a family feud which went on for years. To stop this killing, people were given a 'death-price'. The murderer paid this death-price to his victim's family. A villager's death-price was about £10. If a lord was killed, the death-price was about £600! If the murderer couldn't pay, he went to prison, where his family had to feed him.

Taxes

Landowners paid tax every year, according to how much land they had. If the king had to pay the Danes a bribe to stop them from raiding, people were taxed again.

When a landowner paid a tax, the tax collector made a cut on a wooden stick called a tally. The scribes (writers) copied out the figures for the king from these tallies.

New laws, or announcements, were delivered to the sheriff of each shire by messengers on horseback. This is how the king let his subjects know his plans for them.

A king sits with his Witan. The king's court decided if a person was guilty or innocent.

This is a page from one of Alfred the Great's law books. He sent a copy to all his burhs. The page begins 'This book shall go to Worcester'.

Everyday life

The Anglo-Saxon settlers built wooden houses. They used reeds to thatch the roof. The houses had no chimneys and smoke escaped through the thatch. Women cooked in a big iron cooking pot hanging over an open fire in the middle of the house.

Men and women were either 'free' or 'unfree'. The unfree were slaves. They were given a small piece of land to live on and food in exchange for work. Free peasants owned a 'hide' of land and livestock. A hide was the amount needed to feed a family through the year. A peasant's working day was hard and long. He had to grow enough food to feed his family. He got up at dawn and worked until sunset. At noon, his wife or children would bring him a meal of bread, cheese and ale. One day each week a peasant had to work on his lord's land. The lord also owned the mill where the peasant took his corn to be ground into flour.

Women had to fetch water from the well, feed and milk the cow or sheep and cook the meals. They also had to spin and weave wool to make clothes for the family.

Children gathered food for the family. They collected bird's eggs, trapped small animals and birds and caught fish. In the autumn they picked wild berries. They collected wood for the fire and found out which bits burned the best. They learned the difference between mushrooms and poisonous toadstools.

The family had to work all day in order to survive. At night they slept on straw, under sheepskin covers.

Words, words, words ....

'Combe' means 'valley', 'ham' means 'village', 'ley' is a meadow. Can you think of place names which end like this?

At West Stow, Suffolk, archaeologists found the remains of a whole village of early Anglo-Saxon houses. They copied the houses and halls, and we can now see what a village was like more than a thousand years ago.

These models at West Stow show us how people might have dressed and what their houses looked like. Each house had only one room.

A village was often enclosed by a ditch and a wooden fence. This was to keep out robbers and wolves. Outside the fence was common land, where cattle and sheep grazed. There were also fields, where people grew crops. In some places, the fields were divided into strips. Each man ploughed about 30 strips, in different fields. This allowed everyone to share the good and the bad land.

People living in monasteries grew their own food, but they also needed tinkers (who made and mended pots), cobblers, leatherworkers, potters, silversmiths and blacksmiths. These craftsmen set up stalls outside the monastery and other traders and their customers built houses nearby. This is how a town developed. The first towns were small and there were very few of them.

Towns became wealthy through trade. There were no shops so craftsmen and farmers sold goods in the market place. People could buy food, pottery, jewellery, tools, wooden items, leather, clothes and stones for grinding corn.

It's true!

There were no rabbits in Anglo-Saxon England! They were brought here by the Normans, after 1066. But there were wolves in England, living in packs in the forests. They ate other animals, including sheep, so shepherds hated and feared them. Some kings allowed people to pay their taxes or their fines in wolves' heads.

Food and feasting

Each family baked its own coarse bread made from flour and water. They ate it with soft cheese made from sheep's milk. Bread and cheese were everyday foods for most people. After a bad harvest, bread sometimes had to be made out of acorns instead of flour.

In winter, when food for farm animals was scarce, the weakest animals were killed. Meat could be preserved by salting or smoking over a fire. Salt came from the coast and from salt-pans near Droitwich. The salt-pans belonged to the King and his agents sold salt all over the country. In summer, peas and beans were dried for the winter.

Everybody drank ale made from barley, and mead made from honey.

On special holidays or at harvest time, the peasants went to the lord's hall for a feast. They ate boar's meat and venison (deer) and drank ale. Although food was cut up with knives and served with ladles, people ate with their fingers as there were no small spoons or forks.

A king at a feast. He is being waited on by servants.

Health and healing

Life could be very short. But though many people died before they were 25, a surprising number lived to be quite old.

People used herbs, onions and garlic for mild sicknesses, but these were useless against plague, or sword wounds. Healers often cut a sick person (this was called bloodletting) to let out a fever. The wound often went septic. Many women died when giving birth. When the weather was bad and the crops failed, hundreds of people starved to death.

Everybody believed in witchcraft and magic. People wore charms to keep away illness and bad luck.

A jug used to hold wine or ale. In Anglo-Saxon times, the weather in Britain was warmer than it is today and people were able to grow grapes and make wine.

Take earthworms, pound well, lay on until the cut is healed
An Anglo-Saxon cure for a deep cut

Crafts

The Anglo-Saxons were skilled at crafts. Bronzesmiths and silversmiths made many decorative items and jewellery. They also made useful things like bowls, cups and spoons, armour, knives, spears and swords. Farming tools such as hoes, axes, blades for wooden ploughs and even scissors were also made by smiths.

Wood was used for many things, from building houses to making buckets and cups. Women wove baskets from wooden twigs. Leatherworkers made belts, shoes, horse harnesses, buckets and shields. Pottery jugs, bowls and flasks were made in the towns.

Coloured glass beads were used for jewellery and to decorate clothes.

Clothes

Rich and poor people wore clothes of similar style. Poor people used sheep's wool, which the women spun and wove. Richer people could afford finer linen material, made out of a plant called flax. Most clothes were made at home, by hand.

Clothes had no buttons. They were fastened with metal buckles. Rich people wore gold buckles decorated with precious stones, coloured glass and carved patterns.

Men wore short tunics with a belt, and woollen stockings. In cold weather they added to this a long cloak, fastened on one shoulder. Women wore long dresses with wide sleeves. They covered their heads with a hood.

Both men and women wore leather shoes or sandals, sometimes held in place with leather strings or laces. Leatherworkers also made clothes, belts, horse harness, buckets, and round shields.

Children's clothing was similar to that of adults.

This picture shows what a lord and his family would have worn.

Churches and monasteries

As this picture shows, Bede's monastery at Jarrow is now in ruins. The other buildings were built later.

This little church, at Bradford-on-Avon, was probably built during Bede's lifetime.

The first Anglo-Saxon buildings made of stone were churches and monasteries. Many of our cathedrals began as small churches, for example, Canterbury, York, St Albans and Winchester.

Monasteries were places where scholars, monks and nuns could work and pray. They were usually built in a square around an open space (the cloister). On one side of the square was the church. On the other sides were the refectory (dining-room), a dormitory, library, store rooms and guest rooms. There were separate buildings for cooking and brewing ale.

There were hundreds of monasteries, all over England. They were built near a good water supply and fertile land. One famous one was at Jarrow, Northumbria. It is here that Bede lived and wrote his *History of the English People* (see page 6). He was the greatest scholar of his time. Six hundred monks worked on the farm and in the buildings at Jarrow.

Wealthy women sometimes gave money to build a nunnery. Cuthberga, the sister of King Ine, founded one at Wimborne in Dorset. Hilda, of the Northumbrian royal family, became Abbess (head) of Whitby Abbey in 657. She taught the monks Latin and literature. One of the monks, Caedmon, wrote religious poetry in English, so that the common people could understand what he wrote. Hilda was well-educated and wise. Even kings and bishops asked her advice. Many religious people, including Cuthberga and Hilda, were made saints after they died. People prayed for them on their special 'saint's day'.

Scholar monks borrowed Bibles and psalm books from

other monasteries. They copied them on vellum (very fine sheep or goat skin) and painted pictures and capital letters on each page in bright colours. They bound the books in leather. A book was a very precious object.

The Danes destroyed many of the monasteries. In the 10th century Dunstan, the Archbishop of Canterbury, had them rebuilt. He encouraged young men and women to become monks and nuns once more. They had to follow very strict rules.

Most people could not read or write. They listened to story-tellers, who recited poems and tales about heroes and dragons. One of these poems is about a prince called Beowulf. He fights with human enemies and monsters. At the end he dies. His property is buried with him. The description reminds us of the grave at Sutton Hoo.

This is a page from the Book of Kells. It is a copy of the Gospels, written in Latin. The decoration is so fine that people thought it had been painted by angels. It was written in the 8th century.

They buried rings and brooches in the barrow .... They bequeathed the gleaming gold, treasure of men, to the earth, and there it still remains as useless as it was before. Then twelve brave warriors, sons of heroes, rode round the barrow sorrowing.

Beowulf

Words, words, words ....

'Faeder ure, þu þe eart on heofonum.' is 'Our Father, which art in heaven' in Old English. The letter that looks like a p is pronounced 'th'. The Lord's Prayer was translated into English from Latin during Anglo-Saxon times.

Travellers and traders

Most men and women never left their own shire. To get to the next village, they walked or rode horses along narrow tracks. They took their produce to market in wheeled carts. If they came to a wet and muddy place, they walked round it, so tracks sometimes got lost or changed direction. People could also ride or walk from town to town along roads built by the Romans hundreds of years earlier. Roman roads were very straight and were paved with square stones. Some of our modern roads follow the old Roman roads.

The king himself spent a great deal of time travelling with his court. Many wagons carried his money, clothes and food for the journey. When the king and his courtiers arrived at a lord's hall, the lord had to feed and entertain them.

This 10th century picture shows a servant preparing his master's horse.

Seeking adventure and knowledge

Many people went on pilgrimages to Rome. Bede tells us that King Ine went there.

> **A**t this period, many English people followed this custom, both noble and simple, layfolk and clergy, men and women alike.
>
> Bede

Some travellers brought back pictures, books and fine silk cloth. In France, one bishop saw glassmakers cutting glass for windows. He asked them to come to England to teach English builders.

Travel was difficult and dangerous. The travellers had no proper maps. They were often among foreigners who could not speak English. They rode on horseback to the nearest monastery. The monks showed them the way to the next monastery. The journey to Rome took several months.

This is a copy of one of the first stained glass windows made by the Anglo-Saxons.

Long-distance buying and selling

The traders of England were busy people.
Farmers from villages and settlements sold the
crops they had grown in the new towns.
Craftsmen took their woodwork, leatherwork,
metalwork or pottery to sell at the local market.

Lead mined in Derbyshire was sold all over
Britain. Traders carried salt from places like
Droitwich and Nantwich to areas where salt was scarce.
Goods were bought with silver coins.

Most towns in England were within 10 or 15 miles of a wide
river. Long-distance traders made good use of these rivers.
They could row far up the Humber or the Thames or the
Severn, and many other rivers. Travelling by boat was much
quicker and easier than going by road.

Wide rivers led to the busy ports of London, Southampton,
Ipswich and Norwich. From these towns traders crossed the
sea to sell English goods. When they returned, they sold
imported furs, swords, ivory and woollen cloth
in the marketplaces.

Fearless overseas traders studied the tides
and the dangerous currents and they knew
the sea routes well. They discovered that wool,
cowhide, butter and cheese sold well in
Norway, Sweden and Denmark. They brought
back bronze bowls and gold and silver
jewellery to sell in England.

Traders from Kent sailed to Normandy in
northern France. They returned with glass
bottles and jugs and wine. While in France,
they bought silver bowls and glass vessels from
other traders. These people had brought
them to France from Egypt and the Middle
East. Goods passed from trader to trader over
hundreds of miles. Sometimes, English kings
ate from silver plates that had been made in
Constantinople (now Istanbul, in Turkey) or
had their wounds sewn up with silk thread
from China!

Ships like this carried people and
goods. This boat has sails and also
oars for rowing and steering. The
artist drew the fish to show that the
ship was on the sea.

The first maps were drawn at the end
of the Anglo-Saxon period. This map
shows what the Anglo-Saxons thought
the world looked like.

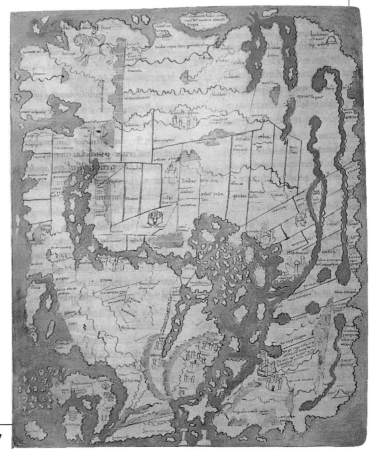

The last Anglo-Saxon kings

Edward the Confessor lived in exile in Normandy, north France, while the Danes ruled England. The people who lived in this part of France were called Normans. When Edward returned as king in 1042, he brought Norman knights and bishops to England. Some were councillors in his court.

The old kingdoms were now ruled by powerful earls. Earl Harold ruled Wessex, and his brother Tostig ruled Northumbria. They hated the Normans in King Edward's court.

Edward the Confessor died in January 1066. He had no son to follow him. Three people wanted to rule England. One was Earl Harold. He said that the dying king had named him as the next ruler. Edward is supposed to have said to Harold, 'I leave my wife in your care, and with her my whole kingdom'. The second was Duke William of Normandy. He said Harold had promised *him* the crown. The third, King Harald of Norway, saw his chance to seize the throne. Tostig, who had quarrelled with his brother, said he would help King Harald.

This part of the Bayeux Tapestry shows King Edward the Confessor. You can see how the picture was sewn.

This silver penny shows King Edward the Confessor.

It's true!

The Normans, like the Danes, were also originally 'Northmen' – Viking raiders. They were given part of north France. By the time they conquered England their language was French.

The struggle for England in 1066

Harold of Wessex was the only one of the three men who was in England in January. He hurried to London and was crowned king. Then the king of Norway landed in the north. Harold's soldiers marched 310 kilometres (190 miles) to York. The English army fought the Norwegians at Stamford Bridge, and won. King Harald of Norway and Tostig were both killed.

Then a messenger arrived. Duke William and the Norman army had landed at Pevensey in Kent. Harold marched his men all the way south again. They had no time to rest. They met the Norman army at Hastings, on the morning of 14th October, 1066. By the time the sun set, Harold was dead.

The Norman duke became King William the Conquerer. The Anglo-Saxon period was at an end.

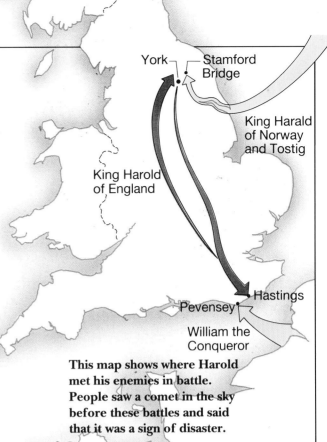

This map shows where Harold met his enemies in battle. People saw a comet in the sky before these battles and said that it was a sign of disaster.

The Bayeux Tapestry

In 1067 English women sewed a very long tapestry in coloured wools. We call it the Bayeux Tapestry (you can see it in Bayeux, France). It is rather like a cartoon strip. It shows how the Battle of Hastings was fought. We can see what people wore, their weapons, and their feasting. King Edward the Confessor is shown with his crown on, and King William the Conquerer in armour. King Harold appears many times. We finally see him being killed by a knight on horseback. Over his head are the Latin words 'Harold Rex interfectus est', which means 'King Harold is killed'.

This is the Battle of Hastings. Notice how many different kinds of weapons the soldiers are using.

Index

Glossary

archaeology   the study of the past, usually by digging up objects buried in the ground

baptism   ceremony in which a person becomes a Christian

blacksmith   iron worker who makes tools, horseshoes etc.

cemetery   burial ground. Many of the Anglo-Saxon objects in museums were found in cemeteries

cobbler   person who makes or mends shoes

Danelaw   northern and eastern part of England settled by the Danes

dyke   ditch with earth wall for defence

fury   rage, violence

Gospels   four books of the Christian Bible

hide   amount of land needed to keep one family

hundred   division of land, usually containing 100 hides

monastery   religious house where monks live and work

oath   solemn promise

pagan   a person who does not belong to any world religion (Christianity, Islam etc.)

prow   pointed front end of a ship

salt-pan   place where salt is obtained, by flooding the land and then letting the water dry out

sceptre   rod carried by a king

tribute   money paid for protection or as a sign of loyalty

Places to visit

Aberlembo (Tayside) – an early stone Christian cross

Barnack (Cambs.) – a late Saxon carving

Bewcastle (Cumbria) – early Christian cross in St Cuthbert's churchyard

Bokerley Dyke (Dorset) – dyke built to keep Anglo-Saxons out of Dorset

Bosham (W. Sussex) – Church of the Holy Trinity. Harold was here before the Battle of Hastings

Bradford-on-Avon (Wilts.) – St Lawrence's Church

Bradwell-on-Sea (Essex) – St. Peters Church founded in 654

Brecon Museum (Powys) – dug-out canoe, etc.

Brompton (Yorks.) – Danish tombstones and cross

Brixworth (Northants.) – All Saints' Church

Carew (Dyfed) – a Celtic carved cross

Deerhurst (Glos.) – St Mary's Church - where Canute met Edmund Ironside

Devil's Dyke (Cambs.) – built between the kingdoms of Mercia and East Anglia

Douglas (Isle of Man) – Viking ornaments and coins

Durham Cathedral Museum – items from St Cuthbert's tomb

Earls Baron (Northants.) – All Saints' Church

Eliseg's Pillar (Clwyd) – a cross in memory of the king who opposed Offa

Escomb (Durham) – St John's Church

Gosforth (Cumbria) – a cross and Anglo-Saxon tombstones

Greensted (Essex) – St Andrew's Church

Hadstock (Essex) – St Botolph's Church

Hexham (Northumberland) – St Wilfred's Church

Jarrow (Tyne and Wear) – St Paul's Church, ruins of Bede's monastery

Kirkdale (Yorks.) – St Gregory's Church, and carved coffin lids

Kirkleavington (Yorks.) – a Danish cross

Laxton (Notts.) – Fields still worked in strips

Lincoln City and Country Museum (Lincs.) – many Anglo-Saxon items

Lindisfarne Island – copy of the Lindisfarne Gospels and other Anglo-Saxon remains

London, the British Museum – the Sutton Hoo treasure

Middleton (Yorks.) – pieces of Danish crosses

Monkwearmouth (Tyne and Wear) – St Peter's Church, and books

Offa's Dyke (Welsh border) – now a long-distance footpath

Ovington (Northumberland) – St Mary's Church tower, crosses

Oxford, the Ashmolean Museum – jewellery, weapons, etc.

Penmon (Anglesey) – Celtic crosses

Reculver (Kent) – ruined church

Ripon (Yorks.) – 7th century crypt

Ruthwell Cross (Dumfries. and Gall.) – cross in apse of church

Sandbach (Cheshire) – a late Saxon carving

Sheffield City Museum – helmet, etc.

Singleton (Sussex) – reconstruction of a house

South Cadbury (Somerset) – remains of a large wooden hall (perhaps Arthur's)

Sutton Hoo (Suffolk) – earthen barrows

Wansdyke (Avon and Wells) – built between the kingdoms of Wessex and Kent

Wareham (Dorset) – one of Alfred's burhs, with the original street plan

Winchester City Museum – brooches etc.

West Stow (Suffolk) – reconstruction of a village

York – the Viking capital, then called Jorvik